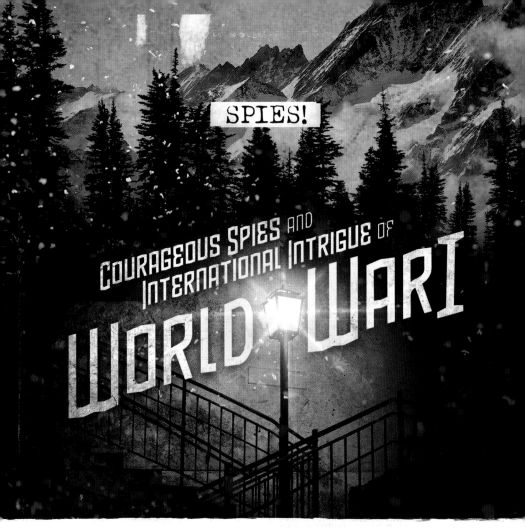

SPIES!

COURAGEOUS SPIES AND INTERNATIONAL INTRIGUE OF WORLD WAR I

ALLISON LASSIEUR

Raintree is an imprint of Capstone Global Library Limited, a company incorporated in England and
Wales having its registered office at 264 Banbury Road, Oxford, OX2 7DY – Registered company number:
6695582

www.raintree.co.uk
myorders@raintree.co.uk

Text © Capstone Global Library Limited 2017
The moral rights of the proprietor have been asserted.

Edited by Megan Atwood
Designed by Russell Griesmer
Picture research by Tracey Engel
Production by Steve Walker
Printed and bound in China

ISBN 978 1 4747 3622 0
20 19 18 17 16
10 9 8 7 6 5 4 3 2 1

British Library Cataloguing in Publication Data
A full catalogue record for this book is available from the British Library.

Acknowledgements
We would like to thank the following for permission to reproduce photographs: Alamy: Chronicle,
24; Flickr: Internet Archive Book Images, 37; Getty Images: Bettmann, 50, Hulton Archive, 13, 30,
Popperfoto, 38; Library of Congress: George Grantham Bain Collection, LC-DIG-ggbain-20235, 22,
LC-DIG-ggbain-07650, 8; Newscom: akg-images, 11, Collection Jaime Abecasis imageBROKER, 49, Everett
Collection, 19, Marcio Machado/ZUMA Press, 6, World History Archive, 29, 40; Shutterstock: Ensuper,
design element, Fedorov Oleksiy, design element, Freedom_Studio, design element, Here, design element,
Nickolay Khoroshkov, cover and 1 (streetlight), phokin, design element, rangizzz, cover and 1 (design
element), Reddavebatcave, design element, SkillUp, design element, STILLFX, design element, Tom
Reichner, cover and 1 (trees), vichie81, cover and 1 (mountains), Vladitto, design element, Ysbrand Cosijn,
cover (male silhouette); The Image Works, Roger-Viollet, 42; Wikimedia: public domain, 14

We would like to thank Joseph Fitsanakis, PhD of Coastal Carolina University for his invaluable help in
the preparation of this book.

Every effort has been made to contact copyright holders of material reproduced in this book. Any
omissions will be rectified in subsequent printings if notice is given to the publisher. All the Internet
addresses (URLs) given in this book were valid at the time of going to press. However, due to the dynamic
nature of the Internet, some addresses may have changed, or sites may have changed or ceased to exist
since publication. While the author and publisher regret any inconvenience this may cause readers, no
responsibility for any such changes can be accepted by either the author or the publisher.

CONTENTS

World War I started with a literal bang – the assassination of the Austro-Hungarian monarch, Franz Ferdinand. But the tensions that led up to the declaration of war had been brewing for decades.

In 1908, Austria-Hungary, worried that its hold in the Slavic region was waning, took over the twin provinces of Bosnia-Herzogovina. Serbia was furious because it considered Bosnia to be part of the Serbian homeland. So Serbian and Bosnian nationalists began a campaign to gain back their homeland.

Meanwhile, France and Russia, angry about Germany taking land from earlier wars, entered into an alliance. Great Britain became a part of this alliance because it was worried about Germany's growing navy. These three powers – France, Russia and Great Britain – became known as the Triple Entente.

Germany had supported Austria-Hungary for years. So when Austria-Hungary's monarch, the Archduke Franz Ferdinand, was assassinated by a Bosnian nationalist, Germany pledged its support to Austria-Hungary. With that support, Austria-Hungary declared war on Serbia in 1914 and what was then known as the Great War began.

The war spanned most of the globe. The Allies included Great Britain, France, Belgium, Italy (which first sided with the Central Powers), Japan, Serbia, and later in the war, the United States. The Central Powers were Germany, Austria-Hungary, the Ottoman Empire and Bulgaria. The empires with colonies enlisted the countries they ruled into the fight, bringing in India, South Africa, Brazil, Canada and many others.

After four long years of battle, the Central Powers began to surrender one by one. Finally, Germany surrendered on 11 November 1918, signing an armistice, or ceasefire. The number of soldiers who died in the war has been estimated at about 10 million. The number of civilians who died is estimated to be between 6 million and 10 million. The war was named "the war to end all wars," but as history teaches, this was not to be. This book tells the stories of a few courageous spies and the international intrigue they navigated during a war that was unlike any other in history.

Gavrilo Princip joined the Black Hand society and became one of its most infamous members.

CHAPTER 1

Gavrilo Princip: The Black Hand and the Start of the War

Gavrilo Princip had to kill himself. He pushed through the crowds that had come to see the heir to the throne of Austria-Hungary, Archduke Franz Ferdinand, drive through the streets of Sarajevo, Bosnia, on 28 June 1914. The archduke and his wife, Sophie, were in the city to dedicate a new hospital. Gavrilo's orders had been simple: assassinate the archduke and then commit suicide. He had failed at the first thing. He couldn't fail at the second.

Gavrilo was a member of the secret Black Hand society, a group dedicated to the unification of the Serbian people. He and six other spy-terrorists had been ordered to the streets of Sarajevo that morning, all with the goal of killing the archduke.

PLANNING THE ASSASSINATION

That spring the head of the Black Hand, Colonel Dragutin Dimitrijević, known as Apis, decided it was time to do something big. The archduke was the future ruler of Austria-Hungary. What better way to fight the hated occupier than to kill its leader? Apis recruited a group of teenagers into the Black Hand, including Gavrilo.

Franz Ferdinand was the archduke of Austria-Hungary.

As a member of the Black Hand society, Gavrilo and the others swore to assassinate the archduke. The Black Hand leaders gave these new recruits guns and grenades, and helped get them to Sarajevo. Then each recruit got something even more deadly: a pill filled with the poison cyanide and orders to commit suicide when the mission was complete.

On that sunny morning, the seven recruits took up positions along the archduke's route. If the first person failed, the job fell to the next, and so on down the line. The archduke's motorcade of six cars left the train station mid-morning and headed to the outskirts of town. This was the moment the Black Hand assassins had been waiting for.

DID YOU KNOW?

The members of the Black Hand worked
together in cells of three to five.
Black Hands didn't know anyone outside
their cells. Each cell got its orders
from a high-ranking leader.

COUNTDOWN TO DEATH

The first Black Hand recruit in line, Mohamed Mehmedbašić, didn't throw his grenade because a police officer was standing nearby. Down the road, next in line, Nedeljko Čabrinović threw his grenade – but it bounced off the archduke's car and exploded under a car behind. Čabrinović swallowed his cyanide pill and jumped into the Miljacka River, hoping to die. But the pill only made him vomit and the river was just a few inches deep, so he didn't drown. Instead, he was quickly arrested.

The archduke's motorcade sped past the other Black Hand assassins one by one. None used their weapons as the cars passed. The crowds were too thick, or there wasn't a clear shot. When the motorcade got to Gavrilo's position, the archduke's car was going too fast for him to get a good aim. Gavrilo was afraid he might accidently shoot an innocent bystander in the tightly packed crowds.

As the motorcade sped away, Gavrilo's heart sank. His gun weighed down the pocket of his coat, and he considered using it on himself. He also had the cyanide. Before he killed himself, he went to a pavement café on a side street and slumped over a table.

A "LUCKY" BREAK

As he was working up the courage to kill himself, the crowds got louder. Gavrilo looked up and saw a stunning sight. The archduke's car had taken a wrong turn into the narrow street. It had stopped, fenced in by the crowds. Sitting in the car was the archduke, not two metres in front of him!

Gavrilo couldn't believe his luck. Slowly he stood up and pulled the heavy gun from his pocket. He fired twice. The first bullet hit the archduke's wife, Sophie, in the abdomen. The second shot hit the archduke in the neck. Screams tore through the crowd. A group of men grabbed Gavrilo and threw him to the ground. He didn't care. The archduke and his wife were dead. He had completed the Black Hand's mission.

The archduke and his wife, Sophie, were assassinated in their car.

THE END OF THE BLACK HAND

Gavrilo and Čabrinović were arrested on the spot. While they were in custody they told police the names of the rest of the Black Hand assassins, and they were soon arrested as well. The only one that got away was Mehmedbašić, who escaped and went into hiding. All the remaining assassins were put on trial. The sentence

EYEWITNESS TO AN ASSASSINATION

Count Franz von Harrach, acting as a bodyguard, was in the car with the archduke and his wife. He wrote down what happened after Gavrilo fired his two shots.

As the car quickly reversed, a thin stream of blood spurted from His Highness's mouth on to my right che[e]k. As I was pulling out my handkerchief to wipe the blood away from his mouth, the Duchess cried out to him, "For God's sake! What has happened to you?" At that she slid off the seat and lay on the floor of the car with her face between his knees. I had no idea that she too was hit and thought she had simply fainted with fright. Then I heard His Imperial Highness say, "Sophie, Sophie, don't die. Stay alive for the children!"

At that, I seized the Archduke by the collar of his uniform, to stop his head dropping forward, and asked him if he was in great pain. He answered me quite distinctly, "It is nothing!" His face began to twist somewhat but he went on repeating, six or seven times, ever more faintly as he gradually lost consciousness, "It's nothing!" Then came a brief pause followed by a convulsive rattle in his throat, caused by loss of blood. This ceased on arrival at the governor's residence.

for murder was death, but these Black Hand spies got lucky. All but one of them were still in their teens. Under the law, because of their age, they could not be executed. Instead, they were all thrown in prison. Gavrilo died of tuberculosis in prison two years later. Others served their time and were released. Only one of the spies, Danilo Ilic, wasn't so lucky. Because he was over 20 years old, he got the death penalty and was executed.

In 1917 the Black Hand was outlawed and Apis and other Black Hand leaders were arrested and executed by Austria-Hungary. But wartime spying was just beginning. Both sides quickly built up their own spy rings. Intelligence gathering and espionage grew into a powerful part of the Great War.

Supporters of Gavrilo Princip attended his trial.

Blinker Hall gathered many different types of
spies for Room 40.

CHAPTER 2

CODE BREAKERS: BLINKER HALL AND THE SPIES OF ROOM 40

It was an ordinary-looking door, just like all the other doors in the British Admiralty building in London, England. The number "40" appeared on the door, along with a small No Admittance sign. What was behind that door? One of the biggest spy secrets of World War I.

The spies who worked in Room 40 didn't carry guns or go on exciting adventures. Their work was more deadly than that. Their job was to decode secret messages sent by the Germans. They had to discover everything the enemy was planning to do. Every secret message they cracked meant dozens, if not hundreds, of people might be saved.

The boss of Room 40 didn't look much like a spy. Sir William Hall was a naval officer with a facial tic that made him blink all the time. Because of it, he got the nickname "Blinker," and it stuck. When the war began, Blinker and other British officers knew they'd need a team of code breakers in order to win the war. Blinker was the head of British Naval Intelligence, which made him the perfect person to be in charge of a team of spy code breakers.

Blinker Hall's code breakers weren't scientists or math experts. Blinker knew that the best code breakers would be talented in a wide range of skills, from history and languages to cyphers and puzzles. Room 40 spies also needed to be fluent in German.

Room 40 spies came from many different backgrounds. There was Frank Adcock, a college professor who specialized in ancient history. Francis Birch was a brilliant historian and a comic actor. Walter Bruford taught German literature. Alastair Dennison was an Olympic athlete who was fluent in German. Frank Cyril Tiarks was a banker and a member of the British nobility. Dilly Knox studied Greek classics. John Beazley was an expert on ancient Greek vases. Nigel de Grey had been a publisher before he came to Room 40. The Reverend William Montgomery enjoyed translating German religious texts.

"Room 40" was actually composed of three cramped rooms. One of the rooms was a small bedroom with a mouse-infested bed. Throughout the war more code-breaking spies joined the team, and by the end of the war more than 100 code breakers worked in Room 40. At first they took turns working in the small rooms. Later the spies got better offices in the Admiralty Building, but they still called their new space Room 40.

Having brilliant German-speaking code breakers was the first step. Now they had to figure out the German war codes.

(CODE) BOOKS TO DIE FOR

The spies in Room 40 had a secret weapon: not one, but three stolen German codebooks! The Allies got the first codebook when sailors from an Australian ship boarded a German merchant ship off the coast of Melbourne, Australia. The British got the second codebook from the Russians, who'd destroyed a German ship in the Gulf of Finland. Sailors from a British fishing boat pulled a lead-lined chest out of the wreckage of a German ship, and inside was the third codebook. All three codebooks made it to Room 40 in the first few months of the war.

The Germans didn't know their precious codebooks had fallen into enemy hands. The spies in Room 40 started using the codebooks as soon as they got them, deciphering hundreds of messages. But using the German codebooks proved to be trickier, and more dangerous, than the Room 40 spies expected. The Allies knew that if they used all the information from the decoded messages, the Germans would quickly realize that their codes had been broken. So Allied forces had to choose carefully which intelligence they used. Sometimes they had to let German attacks happen, sacrificing Allied lives so their code-breaking secrets would be safe.

The Germans eventually changed some of their codes, but that didn't keep the Room 40 spies from breaking them too. The Germans often sent messages in both the old and new codes, so that their armies would be sure to understand them. That was great for the Room 40 spies. They were able to compare the new codes with the old ones to break the messages. Through most of the war they were able to use the codebooks to read thousands of German messages. They even kept track of German armies and naval fleets. This was especially helpful for the Allied forces. When the war started, the Allies spent a lot of time searching the oceans for enemy ships and submarines. They were afraid of surprise attacks. The Room 40 spies could tell them exactly where all the German forces would be. The Allies didn't have to worry about surprise attacks anymore. They could focus their time and energy on fighting.

THE ZIMMERMAN TELEGRAM

The war dragged on for two and a half terrible years. By 1917 millions of soldiers on both sides were wounded or dead. Neither side was winning. Britain had begged the United States to join the war on their side, but President Woodrow Wilson would not do it. Only something really big could convince him to throw the United States into the war.

On 17 January 1917, two Room 40 spies, the Reverend Montgomery and Nigel de Grey, intercepted a coded German message. It used a code they didn't know, but it was similar to other codes they already knew. Slowly they decoded it, one section at a time. The message had been written by the German foreign minister Arthur Zimmerman, and sent to his German ambassador in Mexico, Heinrich von Eckhardt. As Montgomery and de Grey broke each section of the message, they got more excited. This was bigger than

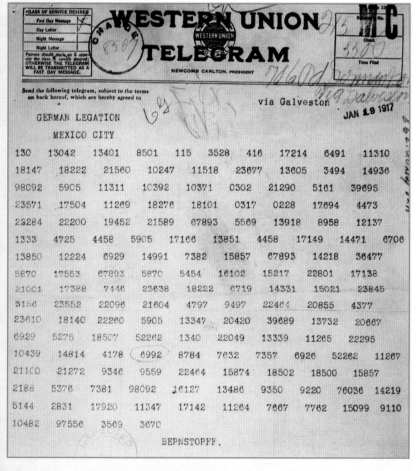

The Zimmerman telegram helped change the course of the war.

anything they'd ever decoded. It was so huge that they didn't even bother cracking the whole message. Instead, they ran to Blinker Hall.

De Grey blurted out, "Do you want America in the war, sir?"

"Yes, why?" Blinker replied.

"I've got a telegram that will bring them in if you give it to them," de Grey replied breathlessly.

Blinker read the half-decoded telegram in shock. The German foreign minister revealed that Germany was going to begin unrestricted submarine warfare. That meant German submarines would attack every ship they saw, including American ships. The ambassador was worried that this might push the United States to enter the war against Germany. So he made Mexico an unbelievable offer. Germany asked Mexico to start a war with the United States, with Germany's help! If Mexico agreed, Germany would make sure that Mexico would get Texas, New Mexico and Arizona back from the United States.

A few weeks later, the Zimmerman telegram and its explosive message got to President Wilson. He was outraged, but he had promised the people of the United States they would not go to war. He gave the telegram to the newspapers, which splashed it all over their front pages. As predicted, people of the United States were horrified. When President Wilson finally called for war, the country was ready to listen. On 6 April 1917, the United States declared war on Germany and entered World War I.

FATE OF ROOM 40

Cracking the Zimmerman telegram was one of the greatest moments in wartime code breaking. The spies in Room 40 continued their work until the war ended in 1918. After that, most of them went back to the lives they had before the war. But peace didn't last long. In 1939 World War II began in Europe, and many of the Room 40 spies went back to work as code breakers in another world war.

Edith Cavell helped hundreds of soldiers escape.

CHAPTER 3

EDITH CAVELL: THE NURSE WHO SPIED

One early summer day in 1915, nurse Edith Cavell and several other nurses were tending the sick and injured in their Red Cross hospital in Brussels, Belgium. Suddenly, shadows darkened the hallway. The German secret police had come looking for Edith. She was a spy, they said. She was a traitor. They searched but found nothing of value and left. Edith had been warned. The Germans were watching.

What did the German army want with a 49-year-old British nurse? Edith Cavell was part of an underground resistance group that helped more than 200 English soldiers escape the German army during World War I.

NURSE TURNED SPY

Edith never expected to become a spy. She grew up in the English countryside and trained as a nurse in Britain. When she was in her 40s, a friend, Dr. Antoine Depage, asked her to travel to

Brussels, Belgium, to nurse one of his child patients. He saw her skill and dedication and asked her to run the first nurses' training school in Belgium, the Berkendael Medical Institute. By the time war broke out in 1914, the Berkendael, under Edith's leadership, was among the best in Belgium.

When the war began, the nursing school was turned into a Red Cross hospital, which had a duty to care for all soldiers regardless of where they were from. Edith's hospital became known as a place where everyone would be treated fairly.

When the German army invaded Belgium, the Belgian government abandoned the country. Germany was now in

Edith Cavell (bottom row, first on the left) ran a nursing school in Belgium.

control of Belgium, and it made some alarming changes. They still allowed Cavell's Red Cross hospital to help everyone, but they ordered that Allied soldiers who had recovered from their injuries had to report to the police. Cavell began to notice that these soldiers were never heard from again. Then on 1 November 1914, two wounded English soldiers, Colonel Dudley Boger and Sergeant Frederick Meachin, appeared at the hospital.

Edith remembered the posters all over Brussels that screamed, "Any Male or Female who hides an English or French soldier in his house shall be severely punished." Edith knew that "punishment" was death by shooting. But she couldn't hand English soldiers over to the Germans. She brought them into the hospital and took care of their wounds. Eventually the soldiers escaped.

Edith used the hospital as a safe house. She would often keep soldiers in the hospital for longer than they needed to be there, to keep them out of German hands for as long as possible. As long as the soldiers were "patients," the Germans left them alone. If the beds were full, Edith put the soldiers in the hospital's attic or cellar. In one year Edith's network saved more than 200 soldiers from the German army.

SECRET MESSAGES

Edith's network also smuggled secret messages to the Allied forces in Britain. Even though Edith and her fellow resisters didn't focus on intelligence, they watched and listened and sent any useful information to the Allies. The soldiers they helped carried these messages – such as the locations of secret German stockpiles of ammunition and gasoline – hidden in the soles of their shoes or in their boots. Sometimes they would write the messages about the locations of German forces and aircraft on handkerchiefs, then sew them into the lining of their clothing.

EDITH'S COVER IS BLOWN

German officers gradually learned about the safe house network Edith worked with. They began secret surveillance of Edith and the nurses who worked with her. Finally the German secret police decided to act.

By then Edith and her fellow spies knew that the Germans were suspicious of them. On that day in 1915 when the German secret police arrived at the hospital, Edith was sure she would be arrested. But one of her nurses, Elizabeth Wilkins, also a spy, saw the soldiers heading to the hospital and immediately realized what was happening. She rushed to Edith's house and hid all the dangerous documents minutes before the Germans arrived. The Germans never found them.

The German secret police detained Wilkins and interrogated her for four hours. She denied any knowledge of a network helping soldiers. Finally the Germans let her go. But they were

DID YOU KNOW?

The International Committee of the
Red Cross (ICRC) was founded in
Switzerland in 1863. Its only purpose,
then and today, is to care for the
victims of wars and armed conflicts
around the world.

on to her and the rest of the spies, and Edith knew it. Edith destroyed all the documents and evidence she had, but she refused to stop spying.

Her friends begged her to leave the country, but she stayed. On 31 July 1915, the German secret police arrested two members of her network. They also confiscated a stack of documents that included the names and addresses of network members. Five days later, Edith and Wilkins were arrested as well. Over the next few weeks, 35 members of Edith's underground network were arrested.

INTERROGATION, TRIAL AND EXECUTION

Edith sat in a dimly lit room, facing her German interrogator. She admitted to helping more than 200 soldiers escape occupied Belgium. "Had I not helped," she said, "they would have been shot."

Edith's trial only lasted two days. She was sentenced to death, along with others in her organization. But no one really thought the Germans would go through with the execution. Edith admitted only to helping soldiers, not to sending messages. The fact that she'd nursed German soldiers along with Allied troops was in her favor too. But the Germans decided to make an example of Edith. They argued that because of her, Allied soldiers lived to fight against the Germans. Alarmed, diplomats from the

United States and Spain stepped in to defend Edith. The Germans ignored their pleas.

Early on the morning of 12 October 1915, Edith was executed by firing squad and unceremoniously buried at the site.

Her death led to widespread outrage, especially in the United States and Britain.

Edith Cavell was given a death sentence for spying.

Thousands of British men enlisted after her death. Books, songs and stories of Edith's bravery and honour swept through Britain and the United States. People saw her as a martyr to the Allied cause. Edith Cavell's execution created a wave of anti-German feeling in the United States, and was one of the reasons the United States finally entered the war 18 months later. When the war was over, her body was returned to England. Crowds lined the streets as the procession bearing her coffin rolled slowly past.

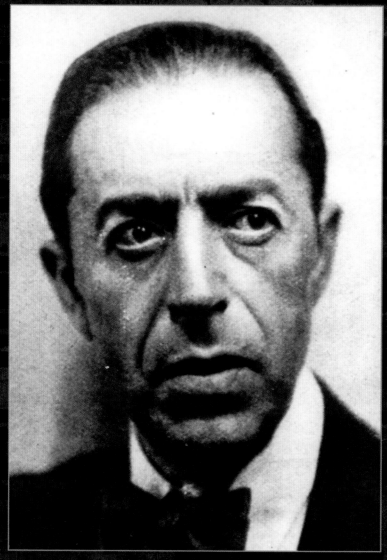

Sidney Reilly was known as a master of disguises.

CHAPTER 4

SIDNEY REILLY: THE ACE OF SPIES

In August 1918, Sidney Reilly, the "Ace of Spies," got some terrible news. Someone had tried to assassinate Vladimir Lenin, the Bolshevik leader of Russia. That wasn't what worried Sidney. The bad news was that he hadn't been a part of it.

Sidney, along with a small, secret group of spies, had been plotting to overthrow Lenin for weeks. If their mission was a success, the Allies would be closer to winning the Great War. If they failed, they would all be executed. The spy group didn't know the person who had attempted the assassination. What Sidney did know was that now his small group had to move fast. As soon as the Cheka, the Russian secret police, started investigating the assassination, Sidney was sure they'd find out about his spies. Their cover would be blown, and their lives lost.

MYSTERIOUS BEGINNINGS OF A MASTER SPY

Sidney Reilly had faced death many times. Or had he? Sidney would go on to have many nicknames including, "Ace of Spies" and "The Greatest Spy in History." But no one knew his real name. At various times he claimed his father was an Irish sea captain, an Irish minister, a Russian aristocrat or a wealthy landowner from Russia. The most likely story – though never verified – is he was born in Odessa, Ukraine, the son of Russian Jewish parents, and his real name was Sigmund Rosenblum.

The stories Sidney told about his early years were so outlandish that most historians today think he made them all up. According to Sidney, he faked his own death to escape Odessa and stowed away on a ship to South America. Then, he somehow became part of an expedition to the Amazon jungle. As if that weren't dangerous enough, he bragged that he single-handedly rescued a group of British officers from a tribe of jungle cannibals. Amazingly, one of the officers just happened to be a member of the British Secret Intelligence Service, known as MI1(c) at the time. The officer was so grateful to Sidney for saving his life from the cannibals that he gave the young man money, a British passport and a job as a spy.

Were these stories true, or cover for a top spy looking to hide his tracks? No one knows. Almost the only thing that can be proven is that Sidney did arrive in London in 1895. By that time he knew several languages, including Russian, German and English. One fact that everyone agrees on is that in 1909, Sidney was hired, unofficially, of course, to spy for the new Secret Intelligence Bureau.

UNDERCOVER AROUND THE WORLD

In the years before World War I, Sidney travelled the world as one of Britain's most covert spies. By all accounts he was elegant, sophisticated and charming – perfect qualities for a spy. Sidney had eleven passports with eleven different identities. He had a reputation for ruthlessness: an agent who would poison, stab, shoot or choke anyone in his way.

One of Sidney's most dangerous missions began in 1909. He had to go undercover and steal plans for German weapons. If he were caught, he would be executed. It is the thought that Sidney went undercover as a German worker at the Krupps weapons manufacturing plant and generously volunteered to work the night shift. Then he broke into the company's secret files and stole plans for the weapons.

When World War I began, Sidney had been spying for Britain for years. But he, along with the other British agents, had worked in the shadows. The British government hid the agents' existence because they didn't want other world powers to know they had a spy organization. That changed in 1918, when the British government officially acknowledged the British Secret Service.

Finally, Sidney was an "official" secret agent, working with the open support of the government. He got a code name, "Agent ST1." Even though the war was almost over, Sidney was about to start the most dangerous mission of his life.

MISSION: DISASTER

In 1917 World War I raged on in Europe. In Russia, the people revolted against the government. The Bolshevik party and its leader, Vladimir Lenin, overthrew the tsarist government in a series of attacks known as the Russian Revolution. Lenin and the Bolsheviks took power in November 1917. One of the promises Lenin made was to withdraw Russia from the war. Britain and the other Allies went into a panic. They feared that if the Russian forces went home, German armies could easily defeat the Allies and win the war.

Many sources disagree on what came next. According to some sources, the British began plotting to overthrow Lenin and put a new leader in his place. The new leader, they hoped, would keep Russian forces fighting alongside the Allies. Eliminating Lenin was a job for the best spy they had for such a task: Sidney Reilly.

Sidney jumped at the chance to complete the mission and was soon in Russia. He made contact with Robert Lockhart, a diplomat and the secret leader of the British spy network there. For weeks in the spring and summer of 1918 a small group of

DID YOU KNOW?

Sidney Reilly and his World War I adventures
are said to be one of the inspirations for
author Ian Fleming's most famous fictional
spy, James Bond.

top spies met in secret and plotted the biggest mission they had ever been given. With the help of their anti-Bolshevik Russian friends, Sidney and the spies would take down Lenin and the entire leadership of the Bolsheviks.

The spies had a bold plan. The Bolshevik leaders were planning a big meeting. First, the spies would make sure all the soldiers assigned to guard Lenin during this meeting were traitors who wanted to overthrow the Bolsheviks. They would bribe the soldiers and other anti-Bolsheviks to attend the meeting. Once all the leaders were inside the meeting room, the guards would shoot Lenin and the other leaders. Sidney and the other spies would be hiding behind curtains with grenades. If something went wrong, they were to use them on the assembled leaders.

They put the plan in place, but almost immediately, things started going wrong. The big Bolshevik meeting was postponed at the last minute, ruining their careful plan. Unknown to them, someone betrayed their group to the Cheka, the Bolshevik police. The Cheka were almost ready to arrest the spies when, on 30 August 1918, a Russian woman named Fanya Kaplan shot and wounded Lenin during one of his speeches. She insisted she acted alone, but the Cheka became nervous. It was time to arrest the British spies.

The British government has denied any involvement in an assassination attempt against Lenin. Some sources say the plot was hatched by a group of Latvian nationalists opposed to Lenin and the Bolshevik movement – that neither Sidney nor Lockhart plotted to kill Lenin. These sources say that the Latvian nationalists set up the British (and were in turn set up by the Cheka). Whatever the story, Sidney escaped only 30 minutes before the Cheka arrived to arrest the British spies. One version of his escape story says he paid 60,000 rubles to a smuggler to get him out of Russia. He finally made it back to London. The Bolshevik government sentenced him to death in absentia. If he ever showed up in Russia again, he was a dead man.

THE SPY WITH ONE HUNDRED FACES

One of Sidney Reilly's fellow spies, and the greatest master of disguise in World War I, was the spy Paul Dukes. His specialty was going undercover in Russia, spying on and sometimes for the Bolsheviks.

SIDNEY'S LUCK RUNS OUT

After the war, Sidney was celebrated by the British for his service and awarded the Military Cross. For a time he lived the life of a celebrity spy. But it didn't last long. He lost money on bad business deals and started asking his spy bosses for money. His bosses got tired of it. They also got tired of Sidney's obsession with the Bolsheviks in Russia. By 1921 the Secret Service had fired him.

Vladimir Lenin led the Russian Revolution in 1917.

By now in the USSR (the union of Russia and other countries under Soviet rule), Lenin was dead and Joseph Stalin had taken his place. Stalin was a ruthless leader who wanted all of the Soviet Union's enemies dead. Sidney was high on Stalin's list. The GPU, Stalin's secret police, set a trap for Sidney. They made up a fake secret group called the Trust, which was purportedly against Stalin. Members of the group contacted Reilly, asking him to join them. Sidney knew there was a risk he was being set up, but he loved taking risks. The GPU arrested Sidney the moment he arrived in the USSR.

No one is sure what happened to Sidney after he was taken prisoner by the GPU. The Bolsheviks said he was killed at the border. Some stories say he was arrested and shot after several days in a Russian prison. One account says that GPU officers killed him in the woods outside of Moscow.

But reports of Sidney sightings continued for years afterward. Though the rumours were probably false, even in death, Sidney's mysteries lived on.

Mata Hari was a world-famous dancer.

CHAPTER 5

MATA HARI: DEADLY SPY OR INNOCENT DANCER?

By the time World War I began, Mata Hari's dancing career was fading. She had been the toast of Europe for years, performing mysterious, enchanting dances for packed theaters. She was beautiful, with long dark hair, dark eyes and an olive complexion. On stage, she moved with a grace and skill that the newspapers called thrilling, exotic and daring. Her gem-encrusted costumes entranced audiences everywhere she went.

In 1914, however, her audiences were mostly gone. The world was at war. Mata Hari needed a way to make money to maintain the lavish lifestyle she had grown used to. Could spying be it?

LOCAL GIRL MAKES GOOD

Mata Hari was the stage name for Margaretha Geertruida Zelle, born in Leeuwarden, Netherlands, on 7 August 1876. Her father, a hatmaker, called her his "little princess" and gave her anything she wanted. Life was perfect until she was 13, when her

parents divorced. She was sent to live with relatives she hated, and
began plotting a way to escape.

When she was 18 years old, the answer came in the
newspaper. Margaretha saw an ad from a military officer looking
for a wife. Rudolf MacLeod was handsome, smart, an officer and
39 years old. Four months after they met, Margaretha and Rudolf
were married. Soon after, they set sail for the Dutch East Indies

Mati Hari married young as a way to escape from relatives.

(now Indonesia), where Rudolf's company was stationed.

Their marriage was a disaster. Rudolf was an abusive alcoholic who had affairs with other women. Margaretha loved to flirt and enjoyed the company of military officers when Rudolf was away. By 1903 Margaretha and Rudolf were divorced. She travelled to Paris, alone, penniless and with no way to earn a living.

MATA HARI IS BORN

Margaretha began inventing "holy" and "religious" dances she would later claim she learned in the Indies. She created scandalous costumes that showed off her body. She booked small performances, and soon word spread of the cultured and elegant dancer. Her audiences grew. The only thing she needed was a name that was as exotic as her dancing. She chose Mata Hari, which meant "eye of the day" in Malay, one of the languages of Malaysia.

For the next 10 years she gave sold-out performances all over Europe and became an international celebrity. At the height of her career she made as much as £32,000 for a single performance. And everywhere she went, she met wealthy men who fell in love with her. She spent time with nobility, high-ranking politicians and military officers from all over Europe. They bought her clothes, jewellery and property, and gave her money to live the lavish lifestyle she loved.

A GERMAN SPY MAKES CONTACT

When World War I broke out in 1914, Mata Hari returned to the Netherlands, but it didn't take long for her to become bored with the quiet life. Her dancing contracts dried up and she needed money. One day someone knocked on her door. Her visitor turned out to be Karl Kroemer, in charge of recruiting spies for Germany. Kroemer asked her to become a German secret agent, for which he would pay her 20,000 francs (about £50,000 in today's money). He explained to her that her fluency in English, French, Dutch and German, as well as her connections with French military officers, would be helpful to the German army.

At first Mata Hari said no. It wasn't enough money. Kroemer sweetened the deal by saying it was just a trial. If she did well, she would get more. He gave her the 20,000 francs, three bottles of invisible ink and the code name "H21."

Did Mata Hari become a German spy that day? Once the money was in her hands, she said she destroyed the invisible ink and never spoke to Kroemer again. There is no evidence that she ever contacted him or spied for the Germans, although she might have passed some rumours to him, knowing they were worthless. But she kept the money.

Mata Hari was still well known, and she didn't try to hide her meeting with Kroemer. It wasn't hard for British spies to quickly find out that Kroemer had tried to recruit Mata Hari. They also knew that she was not married and enjoyed the company of powerful men, at a time when women were expected to be shy and reserved. Her scandalous lifestyle seemed to them a perfect cover for an international spy. So, when Mata Hari left for Paris a few weeks after her meeting with Kroemer, British agents were certain she was off on her first mission. They sent a message to the French secret service. It warned that Mata Hari was a dangerous spy and had to be watched.

MATA HARI, FRENCH SECRET AGENT?

Mata Hari was back in Paris, the City of Light, and loving every minute. What she didn't know was that the French secret service had sent two men, Tartlet and Monier, to follow her. They tracked her every move, stole her post and even broke into her rooms and searched for anything that would prove Mata Hari was a spy.

Georges Ladoux, the head of Deuxième Bureau, the French military intelligence agency, was convinced Mata Hari was a German spy. The fact that Tartlet and Monier never found anything didn't slow Ladoux down. It became his mission to find something – anything – to prove she was spying.

Ladoux came up with a plan to trap Mata Hari. He offered her a job as a French undercover agent. She wanted a million francs for the job, and Ladoux agreed, because secretly he never intended to pay her. Their "plan" was for her to infiltrate the highest levels of the German government, even becoming close to Crown Prince Wilhelm. Then she would pass German secrets to Ladoux. Mata Hari still had many male admirers in the German high command, so this idea sounded good.

As Mata Hari prepared to leave for Germany, Ladoux kept surveillance on her mail, phone calls and everyone she met. He set up the trap even further by contacting the intelligence offices in every country Mata Hari was to travel through, alerting them to the dangerous spy who was on her way.

Mata Hari never made it to Germany. She was detained and searched everywhere she went, just as Ladoux hoped. While stuck in Spain, she met a German officer who gave her some information about the German troops. Frustrated that she couldn't travel to Germany, Mata Hari sent this information back to Ladoux and headed back to Paris. As far as she was concerned, she had done her job and it was time to get paid.

A surprise waited for her in Paris: on 13 February 1917, Mata Hari was arrested as a German spy. Ladoux claimed he'd intercepted several secret German messages about the German spy, "H21", and accused Mata Hari of being that spy. She denied it. But Ladoux had his proof – or so he said.

Mata Hari was convicted as a spy and executed in France on 15 October 1917. To her last day she insisted she was innocent.

INNOCENT OR GUILTY?

Was she, in fact, a secret double agent, blinding her victims with beauty? No one ever found any evidence that she had spied. All of the men who could have spoken in her defence refused to testify at her trial. In any case, everyone was tired of war, and people were ready to hear any news that made them think they were winning. The execution of such an exotic, famous German spy was perfect.

Four days after Mata Hari was executed, Ladoux was arrested as a German spy! His connections in Germany could easily have allowed him to fake the secret German messages about Mata Hari, although no one ever tried to prove it. He was eventually acquitted, but it was the end of his spy career. No one trusted him ever again.

Many years later, the prosecutor in Mata Hari's trial, Andre Mornet, made an astonishing comment. He said of her trial, "There wasn't enough evidence [against her] to flog a cat." Yet he condemned her to death anyway, to serve as an example of what France did to captured German spies.

DID YOU KNOW?

After her death, Mata Hari's head was removed
from her body and given to the Museum of Anatomy,
in Paris. At that time, it was thought that by
studying a criminal's head, science could find
out what caused people to become criminals in the
first place. For years, her mummified head with
its flowing red hair sat in the museum's storage
room, along with more than 5,000 other heads
and body parts. In 2000, the museum began an
inventory of this neglected, grisly collection.
To their shock, Mata Hari's head was gone. No one
knows when it went missing, or who could have
stolen it. Museum officials think the thief was
probably one of her many admirers, who loved her
enough to want a last, macabre reminder of his or
her affection. Her head has never been found.

LEGEND OF THE BEAUTIFUL SPY LIVES ON

Since her death, books, articles, plays, movies and even ballets have been written about the mysterious Mata Hari. Her name is forever linked with "spy," even though she probably was never a spy at all. The whole truth may never be known.

The mystery around Mata Hari lives on.

La Dame Blanche smuggled messages in many ways during World War I.

CHAPTER 6

La Dame Blanche: A network of spies

A German train rumbled across a lonely stretch of Belgium, carrying supplies to the German troops on the front lines. Miles of empty fields and dark woods stretched in every direction. Small villages dotted the railway line. Near one village, two children played near the train tracks. As the train disappeared in the distance, the children ran to the village and reported to their parents what they had seen: how many cars on the train, and which direction it had been going. The children were spies, part of one of the most secret – and most successful – spy networks of the war.

SECRET EYES ON THE GERMANS

Almost as soon as Germany invaded Belgium in 1914, the German forces took over the entire Belgian railroad system. Soon, huge German supply trains crisscrossed the Belgian tracks on their way to battle. The Allies needed to know everything about those trains. The trains' direction and cargo revealed if they were headed to or from the front lines, and what kinds of supplies were being taken from one area to another. When the Germans moved troops, it was usually because they were getting ready for an attack. But the Allies had no way to send enough spies to Belgium to watch every railway line. So Mansfield Smith-Cumming, the head of British Intelligence, gave spy Henry Landau a huge mission: find and recruit ordinary Belgian citizens to become train-watching spies for the Allies.

Landau got to work. First he identified the Belgian towns where the trains ran. It was vital that the spies live as close to the train lines as possible. He hired a handful of seasoned agents who had been working for some time. Their mission was to visit the towns and see which local citizens might make good spies. Henry and his partners identified and recruited hundreds of eager Belgian citizens. He named his network of spies "La Dame Blanche," which means "the white lady" in French.

UNDERCOVER TRAINING

Their main spy job was to identify and count the number of German troops, as well as what divisions they were from. If the Allies knew what types of troops and weapons were being transported, they could predict when and where the German army might attack next.

The recruits learned how to recognize different kinds of train transports. For instance, a train carrying troops would have cookers on the back cars. Cavalry trains were filled with horses and horse cars. Artillery trains carried guns on open, flat cars. The new spies were also trained to observe how the troops looked. What age were they? Where they clean? Dirty? How was morale?

New recruits learned how to write their secret reports so no one would find them. The reports were written with a magnifying glass on tiny, thin pieces of tissue paper. Spies used India ink, which would stand up to being wet or damaged. Once the report was written, they learned to roll it so that it was very tiny and could be hidden almost anywhere.

SMUGGLING SECRET REPORTS

The spies of the White Lady had one mission: watch German troop movements along the rail network and make daily or weekly reports.

They needed a safe and secret way to pass along their messages, and they couldn't know one another's identities. Landau had a name for the sneaky spy system he invented to solve this problem: the "octopus" system. One agent, the Letterbox, who lived in town and received the messages, was the body of the octopus. The field agents in that town were the tentacles. They passed their reports to the Letterbox, but only if it was safe. The agents used secret signs that no one else knew. For instance, a flowerpot in a certain position, or a curtain pulled up or down signaled "safe" or "not safe."

The agents had lots of clever ways to smuggle their messages. They sewed them into their clothing. They hid them in hollow basket handles. Tin boxes with false bottoms worked especially well. They put their messages in bars of soap or in fresh vegetables. Women hid messages in their hair.

The Letterbox agent collected the reports, checked them and then gave them to the passeur, or ferryman, who smuggled them to the Allies. This was an especially dangerous job since the Germans had built a 3-metre-tall (10-foot-tall) electric fence along the border. German patrols guarded the fence every 91 metres (100 yards). Passeurs snuck to the fence at night, dodging the lights and guards. Sometimes they waited for days, hidden, until they saw a chance to slip through.

Passeurs used thick rubber gloves to get through the fence. Sometimes they used a barrel with no top or bottom to shove between the electric wires, allowing them to crawl through the fence. Volunteering to be a passeur was not for the faint of heart. More than 3,000 passeurs were electrocuted during the war.

As the war dragged on, the Germans realized they were being spied on. So they tried to confuse the spies by removing all the badges and insignia from their uniforms. This way, the spies wouldn't be able to identify the German troops. At first the trick worked. Then Landau got an idea. He recruited hundreds of new agents, called promeneurs, or walkers. Their job was to go undercover as regular citizens and

DID YOU KNOW?

Almost 75 per cent of the intelligence
from all German occupied areas came from
White Lady agents.

SECRET AGENT, SECRET PROMISE

Every La Dame Blanche agent swore an oath, promising to
do their duty for their country:

*I declare and enlist in the capacity of soldier in the Allied
military observation service until the end of the war. I
swear before God to respect this engagement, to accomplish
conscientiously the offices entrusted to me, to comply
with the instructions given to me by the representatives
of the Direction, not to reveal to anyone (without formal
authorization) anything concerning the organization
of the service, even if this stance should entail for me or
mine the penalty of death, not to take part in any other
activity or role that might expose me to prosecution by the
occupying authority.*

make friendly conversation with the German soldiers when the trains stopped at rest areas. By mingling and talking directly to the troops, the spies could find out what divisions they were from and where they were headed. No German army ever got past La Dame Blanche without being identified.

DANGEROUS WORK

A spy for La Dame Blanche could be anyone. Men, women and children worked as agents. They were nuns, priests, bankers, teachers, artists and businessmen. Many of the White Lady spy teams were families. Anna Kesseler and her four daughters joined and worked as couriers and Letterboxes.

The Latouche family was one of the best of these teams. The father (a former railwayman), mother and two teenage daughters developed a schedule so the daughters kept watch during the day and the parents took over at night. To avoid getting caught, the family wrote all their reports in code, making their notes look like a grocery list. They used beans to tell the number of German soldiers, chicory for the number of horses and coffee beans for the number of enemy cannons. They hid their lists in hollow broom handles.

In the Arnold family, 13-year-old Gerardine and her little brother would "play" on the rail tracks so they could report everything they saw. If visitors came to the house, the children took over watch duties while their parents were busy.

Train-watching work could be boring and lonely. The tracks had to be watched day and night. One agent, Julie Barnich, watched trains with her brother Adolphe. She wrote, "There is nothing more horrible than long winter nights in a room without light in forced idleness ... fighting drowsiness and fearing to fail in one's duty. The next day, taking up the same life, with nothing, not relaxation, nor distraction to come break the sombre monotony of the existence."

AT WAR'S END

The White Lady spy network was one of the most successful networks of the war. In 1918 alone, the network provided Allied troops with hundreds of pounds of notes, reports and maps of German troop movements. Because of the White Lady network, the Allies knew exactly where the Germans were every day.

When the war ended, La Dame Blanche spies got something that few wartime spies received: recognition. Each received a certificate of honour and the grateful thanks of both Britain and Belgium.

28 June 1914
Black Hand spy Gavrilo Princip assassinates Archduke Franz
Ferdinand of Austria-Hungary

28 July 1914
Backed by Germany, Austria-Hungary declares war on Serbia
World War I begins

1 August 1914
Germany declares war on Russia

3 August 1914
Germany declares war on France

4 August 1914
Germany declares war on Belgium
Britain declares war on Germany
The United States declares its neutrality

10 August 1914
France declares war on Austria-Hungary

12 August 1914
Britain declares war on Austria-Hungary

23 August 1914
Germany invades France
Austria-Hungary invades Russian Poland
Japan declares war on Germany

27 August 1914
Austria-Hungary declares war on Belgium

1 November 1914
Edith Cavell joins the resistance in Belgium

22 April 1915
German spy Karl Kroemer asks Mata Hari to become a German
secret agent

12 October 1915
Edith Cavell is executed as a spy

7 November 1916
Woodrow Wilson is re-elected president of the United States with the slogan, "He Kept Us Out of War"

17 January 1917
Room 40 spies crack the Zimmerman telegram

1 February 1917
Germany begins unrestricted submarine warfare

13 February 1917
Mata Hari is arrested as a German spy

6 April 1917
The United States declares war on Germany, entering World War I

26 June 1917
First US forces arrive in France

15 October 1917
Mata Hari is executed by firing squad

7 November 1917
Vladimir Lenin and the Bolsheviks take over Russia, winning the Russian Revolution

1918
Sidney Reilly gets official government acknowledgment as a spy with the British Secret Service
Summer: Sidney Reilly and other spies plan to assassinate Vladimir Lenin

30 August 1918
Fanya Kaplan tries to assassinate Vladimir Lenin

11 November 1918
World War I ends

GLOSSARY

archduke title of the princes of Austria

assassinate murder someone who is well known

Bolshevik Russian political party that took power in 1917, in favour of the working class seizing power

conspirators people who plan to commit something, usually harmful or illegal, together

cyanide salt of hydrocyanic acid, a fatal poison

espionage spying using human operatives

execution killing someone as punishment for a crime

grisly shocking; horrible

in absentia in the absence of the person involved

martyr person who dies for a belief or cause

purportedly it is said or believed, but might not be certain

recruit to ask someone to join a company or organization; or, a person who has joined a company or organization

Resistance people of an invaded nation who work together to drive out the invaders, often in secret

tuberculosis disease that affects the lungs and causes fever, cough and difficulty breathing

underground secret and done without government approval

Additional Resources

FURTHER READING

The First World War (History of Britain), Henry Brook (Usborne Publishing Ltd, 2014)

Spies of World War I: An Interactive Espionage Adventure (You Choose: Spies), Michael Burgan (Raintree, 2016)

World War I: Spies, Secret Missions, and Hidden Facts from World War I (Top Secret Files), Stephanie Bearce (Prufrock Press, 2014)

WEBSITES

www.bbc.co.uk/schools/0/ww1/25827997
Learn what life was like during World War I.

www.iwm.org.uk/history/first-world-war
Learn all about World War I through articles and photographs.

www.mi5.gov.uk/mi5s-early-years
Find out about the history of the British secret service.

COMPREHENSION QUESTIONS

1. The spies of the Black Hand network hated the government that controlled their people. They were willing to kill a world leader because they believed it would save their country. Did this make them terrorists or patriots? Use the text and other sources to back up your answer.

2. Room 40 spies revealed important information about the enemy, but the Allied armies didn't always use the information to attack German forces. Why wouldn't the Allied armies use all the information gathered from the codebooks? Find two different sources to back up your answers.

3. Many people believe that Mata Hari's only crime was that she was an independent woman with money at a time when such women were looked upon with hatred and suspicion. But what if she had lived in the 21st century? How would she have been viewed today? Would the charges against her hold up in a court in this day and age?

SOURCE NOTES

p. 12, lines 11–27, Hart, Peter. *The Great War: A Combat History of the First World War.* Oxford, UK: Oxford University Press, 2013, p. 24.

p. 20, lines 3–6, Avery, Andrew J. "All the King's Men: British Codebreaking Operations: 1938–43." Electronic Theses and Dissertations. Paper 2475, http://dcetsu.edu/etd/2475, p. 34.

p. 25, lines 9–10, LaValley, Joy. "Edith Cavell: Fragile Martyr." World War 1, http://www.worldwar1.com/heritage/e_cavell.htm

p. 28, line 15, "Edith Cavell's Life & Legacy." Edith Cavell 1865–1915, https://revdc.wordpress.com/edith-cavells-life/

p. 47, line 16, Shipman, Pat. *Femme Fatale: Love, Lives and the Unknown Life of Mata Hari.* New York: Harper Collins Ebooks, 2007, p. 390.

p. 55, lines 3–13, Proctor, Tammy M. *Female Intelligence: Women and Espionage in the First World War.* New York: NYU Press, 2003, p. 89.

p. 57, lines 3–7, Proctor, Tammy M. *Female Intelligence: Women and Espionage in the First World War.* New York: NYU Press, 2003, p. 86.